THROUGH
THEIR EYES

EMPATHY UNLEASHED

Edited By Roseanna Caswell

First published in Great Britain in 2024 by:

Young Writers
Remus House
Coltsfoot Drive
Peterborough
PE2 9BF
Telephone: 01733 890066
Website: www.youngwriters.co.uk

All Rights Reserved
Book Design by Ashley Janson
© Copyright Contributors 2024
Softback ISBN 978-1-83565-584-9
Printed and bound in the UK by BookPrintingUK
Website: www.bookprintinguk.com
YB0598D

FOREWORD

Since 1991, here at Young Writers we have celebrated the awesome power of creative writing, especially in young adults, where it can serve as a vital method of expressing strong (and sometimes difficult) emotions, a conduit to develop empathy, and a safe, non-judgemental place to explore one's own place in the world. With every poem we see the effort and thought that each pupil published in this book has put into their work and by creating this anthology we hope to encourage them further with the ultimate goal of sparking a life-long love of writing.

Through Their Eyes challenged young writers to open their minds and pen bold, powerful poems from the points-of-view of any person or concept they could imagine – from celebrities and politicians to animals and inanimate objects, or even just to give us a glimpse of the world as they experience it. The result is this fierce collection of poetry that by turns questions injustice, imagines the innermost thoughts of influential figures or simply has fun.

The nature of the topic means that contentious or controversial figures may have been chosen as the narrators, and as such some poems may contain views or thoughts that, although may represent those of the person being written about, by no means reflect the opinions or feelings of either the author or us here at Young Writers.

We encourage young writers to express themselves and address subjects that matter to them, which sometimes means writing about sensitive or difficult topics. If you have been affected by any issues raised in this book, details on where to find help can be found at *www.youngwriters.co.uk/info/other/contact-lines*

CONTENTS

Alderwood Senior School, Aldershot

Emily Shannon	1
Kahlan Crouch (13)	2
Holly Dunkley (12)	3
Sienna Mullen (13)	4

Bedford Girls' School, Bedford

Ella Morgan-Jones (12)	5
Harnoor Sibia (12)	6
Sophie Ballard (12)	11

Bolton Muslim Girls' School, Bolton

Aafiyah Amla	13
Safaa Patel (14)	14
Rabia Raqib	16
Hadia Ahmed (13)	18

Bourne Community College, Southbourne

Rafferty Child-Glue (12)	19
Violet Budgen (11)	20
Jake Kirwan (11)	22
Charlie Goble (12)	23
Hattie Hadden-Burr (11)	24
Amelie Edwards (11)	25
Mikey Babb (11)	26
Isla Conroy (11)	27
Lucian Mikic (11)	28
Savannah Twine (11)	29
Ivy Owen (12)	30
Zachary Denman (11)	31
Finley Williamson (12)	32
Louis Smith (12)	33

Seb Page (12)	34
Lilly Shearman (11)	35
Skyla Hynek (12)	36
Lily Treagus (12)	37
Millie Gray (12)	38
Imogen Caulkin (11)	39
Oliver McFarlane (12)	40
Wills Page (11)	41
Xander Watson (12)	42
Lucas Russell (12)	43
Gian Thapa (11)	44
Layla Overton (12)	45
Ben Farndell (11)	46
Kelsang Tamang (12)	47

Bruern Abbey Senior School, Chilton

Charlie Thomas (14)	48

Chiltern Way Academy, Prestwood

Kaiden Bolton (13)	50
Alfie Hobbs (14)	51
Freya Wakefield	52
Harrison Osborne (13)	53
Ben Wilson (14)	54

Clare Lodge, Glinton

Daisy Soppelsa (17)	55
Darcie Taggart	56

De Aston School, Market Rasen

Claire Olajide (14)	57
Isabel Hernon (12)	58
Charlotte Perkins (12)	59

Ben Kennedy (14) — 60

Etonbury Academy, Arlesey

Amelia Parker (12) — 61
Hannah Olkes (14) — 62
Charlotte Jarvis (11) — 63
Ella Greaney (14) — 64

Horbury Academy, Horbury

Mateusz Iwanicki (11) — 65

International Community School London, Paddington

Michelle Evboifo (12) — 66
Delilah Fabian (11) — 67
Connie Corfield — 68
Melania Hamrick (11) — 69

Islwyn High School, Oakdale

Cari Hicks (12) — 70
Rohan Lewis (12) — 72

Milne's High School, Fochabers

Lauren Murray (16) — 73

New River College Medical, London

Lily Bertram (15) — 74

R.E.A.L Education, Mansfield

Erin Young (17) — 75

Royal Greenwich Trust School, Greenwich

Aliyyah (13) — 78
Destiny Njoku (12) — 80
Samira Yakubu (12) — 82
Chisom Elemide (13) — 84
Neave Foster (11) — 85

Tofunmi Ayeni (12) — 86
Sonela Seferi (13) — 87
Grace Igglesden (11) — 88
Kristi Igglesden (11) — 89
Fadesewa Afeni (12) — 90

Sharples School, Bolton

Felicity-Jo Thornton (15) — 91
Muzen Shenaif (16) — 92
Aqsa Alli (11) — 93

St Anselm's College, Prenton

Patrick Gambles (17) — 94

St Patrick's College, Dungannon

Leona Belo — 96
Ana Maria Baptista Amaral — 97
Teagan Gildernew — 98

The Petersfield School, Petersfield

Amelie Loveday (14) — 99
James Landrum-Patton (14) — 100
Josh Marchant (14) — 102
Rubie McIntyre-Lamek (13) & Charlotte — 104
Mika Valdivia a l'Onions (14) — 106
Kayleigh Skipp (14) — 108
James Kentish (14) — 110
Joe Tully (14) — 112
Nia Lovat Pugh (13) — 114
Izzy Oleary (14) — 115
Ronnie Bradley (14) — 116
Willow Perring (14) — 117
Frankie Ruffle (14) — 118
Harrison Granton (13) — 119
Delilah Carr (13) — 120
Reuben James (14) — 121
Darcey Tebbutt (13) — 122
Ellie Barnett (13) — 123
Maryam Jones (13) — 124
Ryan Chiverton (13) — 125

Maisie Taylor (14)	126
Rose Pinnick (13)	127
Evelyn Macdonald (13)	128
Ella Cooper (14)	129
Oliver Wedley (13)	130
Adriannah (13)	131
Megan Bibb (14)	132
Karla Miu (14)	133
Lola Payne (14)	134
Joshua Huffer (14)	135
Mia Humphries (14)	136

Townley Grammar School For Girls, Bexleyheath

Olivia Eze (13)	137
Chanel Tumasang (13)	138
Martha Brown (12)	140
Shaelyn Rayna (12)	142
Deetya Tiwari (13)	143
Maya Jheeta (12)	144
Elise Kennard (13)	146

Ysgol Brynhyfryd, Ruthin

Eva Topham (13)	147
Maya Venkat (12)	148
Sonia Wasela (12)	149
Ethan Mould (12)	150

THE POEMS

The Tree

In the heart of the park, I stand,
With roots that hug the earth's soft land.
Squirrels hide their treasures in my soil blanket,
Children climb, as they drop their jackets.

People seek my shade so wide,
Beneath my boughs, they find a guide.
The wind whistles through my leaves so green,
In this gentle haven, life's scene.

Picnics spread upon my green floor,
Families gather and love they pour.
And when life's journey reaches its close,
I cradle ashes, a sad repose.

In the park's embrace, I remain,
A silent witness to joy and pain.
In every season, I stand tall,
A symbol of life's rise and fall.

Emily Shannon
Alderwood Senior School, Aldershot

When I'm Gone

When I'm gone, look out at the trees,
Look at the leaves swaying in the cold breeze,
Think of me when I dreamt,
The biggest popstar you ever said.

As you bake, remember our summer trips to your parent's lake.
Memories that will never break.
When hanging out with friends will you get deja vu?

When I'm gone don't you cry a single drop,
But I just can't imagine though, how you could be so okay...
Now that I am gone.

When I'm gone, don't fall in love with somebody that quickly,
I hope you're happy but not like how you were with me.

Kahlan Crouch (13)
Alderwood Senior School, Aldershot

Painting The Colours Of English

Young minds that need to be filled
Shall be filled with my words and wisdom
From Shakespeare to Steinbeck
I bring literature to life

I inspire young minds
To love and appreciate
The beauty of the written word
And the power of reading

For I know that through words
Anyone can change the world
It is a power held in our hands
And we can influence with our voice

So let me teach these students
To create a story or poem that ignites
To believe that anyone's words
Can change anything
And to help bring literature to life.

Holly Dunkley (12)
Alderwood Senior School, Aldershot

Windowpane

Raindrops on my windowpane
In a world of emotions where everything feels the same.
Driving through my memories in my mind's rearview
Living in a story just like she used to do
Mirror reflections mascara stained eyes
In the lyrics of our lives where truth never lies
So here is a poem, a page from my diary
In the melody of heartache, where feelings run free
Like Tina Turner breaking through the pain
I'll speak my truth, let it pour like the rain.

Sienna Mullen (13)
Alderwood Senior School, Aldershot

Robots

Robots are my friends!
But the other way around, I guess it depends.
If my friends died, it would be my end,
But if a robot died, I would rebuild like a trend.
The difference? I don't see.

I love robots, AI, and a lot more
But not long ago, there was a war
And I promised my friends, I swore,
To never misuse androids, so war won't be knocking on our door.
But... would it hurt so much to just investigate?

Although curiosity is not always beautiful,
Nevertheless, imperfections are suitable.
And a pull is dragging at my hair,
Do I give in? Will it cost my air?

Ella Morgan-Jones (12)
Bedford Girls' School, Bedford

Swim To Freedom

I've told many about my story but not this way
Not in the way you would have seen on TV
Not in the way you would have read in a book
This is the tale of the most challenging part of my life

I was only thirteen years old when this happened
This changed my life
For as our country was torn apart in two
While the civil war raged on
My house went up in smoke crying ashy tears as it left this world
I couldn't go to school
I couldn't be a normal teenager at all
For the dangers were too great
When I swam, I swam my heart and left the heavy burdens behind
I couldn't live like this anymore
I had to go
For my dad
For my mum
For Shahed
Only me and Sara could go

We left with my cousin
My heart wept as I left my family behind to face the unknown
I will see them again

I reassured myself
We set off and began our journey
We were refugees now
But I am still the person I was before
The word 'refugee' doesn't change me
I am still me

We battled the sea
Its waves splash on us
Draining our lives
As I swam other refugees to a place called safe
I wouldn't let anything stop me
Not even the sea
I have experienced many things but not like this
Not the blood-curdling screams of people on a tiny boat
Not the pleading of others for mercy
Not the wish to be back home
But I carried on
My life couldn't end like this
I am still me

As I made it to dry land
The land that grew with hopes and dreams
Trampled by many
Achieved by few
I hoped that I would be able to achieve mine
Mine was to swim beside others at the Olympics
Mine was to be safe

Mine was to find a place called home
Mine was to be with my family again
But the journey wasn't easy
For as we walked across different lands of different countries
The dangers grew greater
Our number dwindled
We were tricked and scammed and of what little we had left
I felt like I wanted to crumble and die
I felt like my dreams were being crushed
But I couldn't let that stop me
I am still me

When I reached Germany everything felt brighter
My hopes were raised
I trained and I trained
With the help from a new friend
My Olympic dream was coming true
Even though my journey still haunts me
The drowning
The death
The war
But as I reassured myself, I was lucky
I am lucky to live
I am lucky to make my dreams come true while not many do
I am still me

I got the news that I was competing in the Olympics
My stomach lurched with happiness
I dreamt of one day swimming for my country
At first, I was reluctant to be part of the Refugee Team
But I told myself
A name doesn't change anything
I worked and I worked
I hoped and I hoped
And finally, the day came
I am still me

As I got in my lane
Breathing heavily
I could remember my chat with Sara
She also had a dream to fulfil
So did I
When I started to swim I put everything in it
I swam and I swam and left my sorrows behind
I carried my hopes with every stroke I put in
When I looked up at the board my heart throbbed
My heart lifted with joy
I felt like I could do anything
I jumped up and down
My tears of joy splashed in the water
I am still me

You can do anything
Dreams do come true

My dreams came true
So will yours
I have faith yours will too
Because I am me.

Harnoor Sibia (12)
Bedford Girls' School, Bedford

Deforestation

The snow crunches beneath my paws,
White flakes fall from the sky,
Mice scuttle into their small burrows,
Icicles form on the tree branches,
The frozen river begins to crack.

The freezing wind swirls around me,
Crows circle the clearing,
I trot back to my small hollow tree stump,
A robin hops forward and chirps at me,
I curl up my tail covering my nose,
Slowly my eyes close.

I wake up enjoying that memory,
My legs ache and I lift my head gloomily,
That snowy forest was gone,
Now giant cars dart around me,
Humans hurry across concrete paths,
I whimper and push myself up.

I gag as a detesting smell hits my nose,
The scent of fear covered every corner,
Sickness plagued the area,
Everything was a shade of miserable grey,
A muted plea comes from all the plants,

Another day begins,
My paws bleed on the large road,

Smog covers the sky,
Humans plod into their huge homes,
A tear forms on my matted fur,
And the only thing keeping me alive,
Is the hope that one day,
The forest will come back.

Sophie Ballard (12)
Bedford Girls' School, Bedford

Beauty's Deception

(From the perspective of an insecure boy.)

In the mirror's silent judgement, I stand
A boy convinced beauty slipped through his hand.
"Handsome," they say, but my reflection denies
In the cavern of doubt, where my confidence lies.

Eyes that see flaws in the canvas of skin
A heart imprisoned, where self-love is thin.
Despite accolades and compliments arrayed
I wear a mask of sorrow, beauty betrayed.

Invisible scars etched on this handsome façade,
A soul's silent scream in a work applaud.
Mirror, mirror, can't you see
The pain of an insecure boy longing to be free.

In the silence, I plead with the mirror's glass
Hollow applause, as my self-worth does amass
Each invisible scar, a whispered plea
I, an insecure boy, yearning for empathy.

Aafiyah Amla
Bolton Muslim Girls' School, Bolton

In Palestine's Land!

In Palestine's land where bombs rain down,
Suffering souls in rubble are found.
Families torn apart, searching in despair,
Under the debris, their loved ones they share.

The smoky, dusty air fills their lungs,
As they struggle to breathe, their spirits are unsung.
Through the chaos and pain, they stand strong,
Their resilience shines, against all wrong.

In Palestine's land where bombs rain down,
Suffering souls in rubble are found.
A woman, her son's blood on her hands,
Cries in anguish, a heart that understands.

She clings to the stain, won't wash it away,
For it's the only remnant of her child's stay.
In her tears, a mix of sorrow and pride,
A mother's love, forever undenied.

The dusty air, heavy with despair,
Engulfs the land, a constant nightmare.
But amidst the chaos, a spirit prevails,
Strength and unity, their story entails.

In Palestine's land where bombs rain down,
Suffering souls in rubble are found.
In the depths of sorrow, a tale unfolds,

Of a man burdened with grief, untold,
Two bags he carried, heavy with despair,
His children's lives lost, trapped in the snare.

Beneath the rubble, their innocence lay,
A tragic fate that no words can convey.
His heart once beating now ceased to beat,
As he crumbled over the weight of defeat.

In Palestine's land where bombs rain down,
Suffering souls in rubble are found.
In a world so innocent, two girls did play,
Unaware of the darkness that loomed that day.

Little did they know, a storm was near,
A bomb dropped from above,
Filling their hearts with fear.
In an instant, their world turned upside down,
As chaos and destruction tore through town.

Their giggles were silenced, replaced by cries,
The little one looks back and the other dies.
Two precious souls taken far too soon,
Their innocence shattered, under the moon.

But let us not forget their resilience and might,
Their spirits unyielding, shining through the night,
For in their hearts, a flame of hope still burns,
Yearning for a future, where peace returns.

Safaa Patel (14)
Bolton Muslim Girls' School, Bolton

In Their Stead

Lies, lies are all she can hear around herself.
Promises, promises she knows are bound to be broken.
An ounce of happiness is all she asks for.
All these years that are passing by her
Before her very own eyes.
She has come to know the true meaning of sadness
and misery.
It is when you destroy yourself with your very own hands.
Expectations ruined her whole life.
All the eyes were on her, making it hard to breathe.
All these voices in her head.
Screaming. Screams of sorrow.
It is all she hears.
While she paints a thin layer of happiness over her face.
On the brink of breaking down, she manages to smile.
All those high entitlements they want her to achieve.
She thought that was what broke her.
At least, that was what she had forced her brain to believe.
No, it was her.
Her and only her.
She raised her expectations of others without realising.
Making the same mistake without noticing over and
over again.
Being broken over and over again.
She, herself, is the only one that stops herself from
feeling anything.

She wishes to no longer exist.
She wishes she hadn't ever tread upon this earth.
Upon her arrival, they hadn't known what she would become.
But she saw herself becoming who she is today.
And if she could tell them, show them.
She would.
That this is, should and will, be, their biggest regret.
This foreign stifled feeling she is now aware of.
This feeling of being on edge.
Of wanting to be everything yet being unable to.
Would the pain end if she ceased to exist?
If she were to sleep forever,
Would the pain be passed on to someone else?
Would they miss her?
Or was she overestimating the feelings of sorrow
This society would endure for her upon her leaving this earth?
She used to feel pity for the dead
And now she's sitting in her own bed writing this.
Shedding unrequired, unnoticeable tears.
Wanting the same fate.
She wishes she was there, dead, in their stead.

Rabia Raqib
Bolton Muslim Girls' School, Bolton

Mother In Gaza

Winter is coming,
Israeli defence forces also,
This pain is numbing
Not just me,
But everyone is filled with sorrow.

How to survive,
Or at least provide for my child,
A roof over one's head,
Rather than on, with them dead.

My child is starving,
My eyes are closing,
But it is not yet spring,
My life is nearly ending.

I don't want to leave my kin,
And I hope one day they will grin,
But for now, winter is coming,
Israeli defence forces also.

Hadia Ahmed (13)
Bolton Muslim Girls' School, Bolton

Messi

My talent is as a footballer
And my family is charming.
I'm very passionate about football,
And I love my family to bits.

Even though I'm miniature,
I don't let anything get to me
Because it will ruin my gameplay
And it will get me frustrated.

I have got the most Ballon D'ors, which is 8.
I have won the World Cup once
And the Champions League many times
And the Golden Boot a bunch.

Something memorable to me
Is my family because they look after me,
And I adore playing with them
Because they are really hilarious and amazing.

I'm one of the outstanding and greatest footballers in the world.
The key is talent, it's nothing without hard work
You can't give up; you have to believe in yourself.

Rafferty Child-Glue (12)
Bourne Community College, Southbourne

My Parents

    M y mum tries to stay strong.
 yo **U** are here to support me, Mum
    M ums are an older version of you

I try to be strong but sometimes I find it hard.
I have been through a lot in the past 2 years because of Covid.
I had long-term Covid
And I still don't feel as strong as I used to be,
But I try not to show it on my face.
My back and my head have been hurting a lot these past months,
But I am struggling to stay strong.
I have to enjoy the times with our family.

    D oing a lot of stuff with my children
    A nd I try to spend less time at work and more with my children
    D ads are important.

I spend a lot of time at work,
But I do go to work to keep our house
Because it is a lot of money,
And I promised my daughter that I would buy a dog,
But that is really expensive,
And I can't break the promise,
And I will never break one

Because I feel like I'm hurting the ones I love.
I will do everything and anything for my family.

Violet Budgen (11)
Bourne Community College, Southbourne

I Am A Blossom

I am a blossom, I'm small and bright,
I bob gently through the light,
I float freely through the breeze,
I have no control but am quite at ease.
My existence is eternally endless,
I'm alone and empty and friendless,
But I am happy to endlessly glide,
Over the rocks and the rising tide.

Now down past the trees where once I sat sweetly,
Till the harsh wind picked me up and stole me.
Now I am simply a pawn in its game,
Swishing down in the thundering rain.
And my world sinks as I drop to the ground,
Without as much as a tinkling sound,
I come to lay on the top of the crest,
Now, I may finally rest.

Jake Kirwan (11)
Bourne Community College, Southbourne

Rock

I am a rock, lonely and scared,
Nobody else would really care.
I am scratched, I am cracked, I am buried in the mud.
The rain is so heavy, the wind is so rough.
The sea is growing.
It is coming so fast;
It's filling my home, my base, my turf.
I sink to the bottom,
I think it is fair to say I have hit rock bottom.
A crab lay sleeping on my smooth surface.
It gave me a warm fuzzy feeling
Like I am not alone anymore.
The sea moves me forward
I fall into a hole
I feel just like I did back home!
But this time, I feel happy and not lonely.
I am a rock, not lonely and not scared.

Charlie Goble (12)
Bourne Community College, Southbourne

My Awesome Pets

    M y
      I nvincible
      L uck
 sc **O** res again

I am Milo and I always bring my owner joy
Day in and day out, 24/7.
Until I was taken on a walk,
I broke my leg and gone from my family's sight,
Gone from my family's perspective.
Even though I am gone from their sight,
I will always be with them in their hearts and heads.
I love them.
They were my whole world.

    M y
      I nvincible
      L uck
 sc **O** res again.

Hattie Hadden-Burr (11)
Bourne Community College, Southbourne

Siblings

B rave, brainy and kind
R esting 24 hours a day
O ther than being annoying
T he rain doesn't stop
H anding in homework
E ating anything I can
R AF

A lways amazing
N ever right
D aring to talk back

S taying out late
I nto the sea
S taying at home
T oo much homework
E ating lots of KFC
R eading nothing
S laying on Fortnite.

Amelie Edwards (11)
Bourne Community College, Southbourne

Chicken

BBQ chicken.
Chicken burger.
Roast chicken.
Fried chicken.
Korean chicken.
Chicken chow mein.
Orange chicken.
Chicken curry.
Chicken goujons.
Chicken nuggets.
Chicken pie.
I love chicken
Because I am a chicken.

I lived in a freezer for many a day
Until someone took me out again
Put me into the oven
And swallowed whole
After some time
I was dropped into the bowl!

Mikey Babb (11)
Bourne Community College, Southbourne

Daffodil

What am I?
Where am I?
All I see is colours,
And things that look like me.

What am I?
Where am I?
My petals are blooming,
My life is beginning.

What am I?
Where am I?
Someone is coming,
And a storm has risen.

What am I?
Where am I?
It's dark,
And they are standing right there.

What am I?
Where am I?
I am no longer attached,
I am lying on the ground.

I am a daffodil.

Isla Conroy (11)
Bourne Community College, Southbourne

The Life Of The Ammonite

I feed, I feed, I float, I swim, I see, I hide, I live.
I see a great light growing.
It slams into the shallow shore,
Where land rises and the sea has little deep.
The light makes a sphere.
The sphere grows.
The sea sizzles.

I no longer feed, there is no food.
I no longer feed, I sink.
I no longer swim,
The great leviathans
Sink with me.
My sight is sore.
I no longer need to hide
I die.

Lucian Mikic (11)
Bourne Community College, Southbourne

Wolves

My paws softly pad on the forest floor.
The sound of crickets surrounds my ears as I prowl.
I open my jaw and howl at the glowing moon.
I am a wolf.

I run as the rain drips off my coat.
My pupils dilate as my ears prick up.
My vivid green eyes shut.
I am a wolf.

The trees are blurry around me.
The wind whistles in my ears
The pack howls.
We are wolves.

Savannah Twine (11)
Bourne Community College, Southbourne

The Ocean

T he hot days, a plague of people jump around like a swarm of crickets.
H ello winter, I missed you so.
E veryone calms for the cold season

O r so I thought, the
C rashing waves didn't scare the humans off this year
E veryone came tumbling down into the water, no
A ppreciated calm winters
N o time to sleep.

Ivy Owen (12)
Bourne Community College, Southbourne

Blue-Tac Man!

Getting stretched every way
Starting to look like another day.
Fighting others
Sometimes my brothers.
Fight villains
Some are named Dylan.
I stretch and I stretch until I can't anymore
It doesn't matter what's left in the store.
I am Blue-Tac Man, the stickiest and stretchiest being.
Don't mess with me or things will get messy.

Zachary Denman (11)
Bourne Community College, Southbourne

Driftwood

Driftwood, driftwood, cold and bare,
When I am seen, people just don't care.
Little do they know my history long?
From a boat to the water all went wrong.
Crashing out my journey had begun,
Across the oceans; all were fun,
Up and down the choppy sea,
Off that boat, I feel more free.
Falling up on the shore,
My journey ends with no more.

Finley Williamson (12)
Bourne Community College, Southbourne

The Little Flower

F loating through the wonderful wind am I.
L eaving behind a trail of petals
O r a beautiful aroma.
W hen I'm hiding on the floor, I am absorbing carbon dioxide.
E xiting the ground and entering the sky am I.
'R ooting' for my 'buddies'.
Y ou never know what secrets a flower holds.

Louis Smith (12)
Bourne Community College, Southbourne

Wildlife Poem

W ildlife is endangered,
I n the depths of the ocean to the tops of the trees,
L urking and waiting for predators to pass,
D ying and fighting to survive,
L urking in the shadows,
I nvisible to predators,
F ighting to survive,
E ndangered and scared, we are endangered animals.

Seb Page (12)
Bourne Community College, Southbourne

Family

M y job is to be caring all the time
U tterly very helpful
M e and my daughters and sons are very close

A nd we always go shopping
N ever wrong
D elighted to spend time with my children

D aughters always talk back
A lways right
D edicated.

Lilly Shearman (11)
Bourne Community College, Southbourne

My Cat, Coco

M y mother says I'm naughty,
Y es, I know I'm naughty but not all the time!

C an I have some food?
O f course, I love them!
C an you play with me?
O nly then take my heart!

Skyla Hynek (12)
Bourne Community College, Southbourne

The Ocean

O ctopus floating away from the fish.
C rumbs are being dropped on the ground.
E choes from the people investigating deep caves.
A ctivity going on in the sea.
N ear the sea sunbathing.

Lily Treagus (12)
Bourne Community College, Southbourne

Daylight

What am I?
Where am I?
All I see is things that look like me.
I am getting battered and blistered.
I have no shelter,
I feel alone,
I am scared,
I don't want to be seen.
I am a flower.

Millie Gray (12)
Bourne Community College, Southbourne

Stone Alone

S tone stays still on the shining beach.
T rees as tall as giraffes around me.
O ver the rocks, I can see the relaxed sea
N o one to play
E veryone has a friend but me.

Imogen Caulkin (11)
Bourne Community College, Southbourne

Life Of An Eagle

E merge from the frosted peaks.
A cross the world, I travel.
G rip my prey, and carry away.
L ike a jet, I soar through the sky.
E verywhere I go, I always take flight.

Oliver McFarlane (12)
Bourne Community College, Southbourne

Football Crazy

Laughing at the opposition
As I knee slide to the corner flag,
Amazing fans chant
Paddie, Paddie Lane
Never misses a goal,
Everyone loves Paddie Lane
He's the best Pompey player ever.

Wills Page (11)
Bourne Community College, Southbourne

Historic

H ome sweet home; the dinosaurs roam
I n the volcano
S ome eggs lay
T he purple portal
O pens
R ight
I n the
C entre of the volcano.

Xander Watson (12)
Bourne Community College, Southbourne

A Day In The Life Of A Rock

I am a rock
I lay still
On the shore
Waiting, waiting,
And waiting some more.
I wait for the sea
To sweep me away.
I am a rock
Laying still.
Waiting, waiting,
And waiting some more
I am a rock.

Lucas Russell (12)
Bourne Community College, Southbourne

Ocean Poem

For millions of years,
I've been going on
Many have been saved
But others have drowned
I am soft but rough at the same time
I drown the beach with seaweed.

Gian Thapa (11)
Bourne Community College, Southbourne

Bugs

B ugs get the fright of humans coming.
U nderstand where people go and come.
G rateful for everything.
S pecial to have bugs everywhere.

Layla Overton (12)
Bourne Community College, Southbourne

Camels

C onsistently ridden by tourists
A lways spitting
M oreover lazy
E gypt is home to camels
L ightly treading sand.

Ben Farndell (11)
Bourne Community College, Southbourne

Petals

My petals are plum and petite,
I continue to grow peacefully,
Until I was snatched and torn,
Now I lay lifelessly,
Waiting until I am reborn.

Kelsang Tamang (12)
Bourne Community College, Southbourne

I Have Given Up

It is me, Earth, who you stand on,
I was here for you to live on,
Not to destroy,
I have seen what you have done,
The war the battles the destruction,

I fought so much,
But can't any more,
You destroyed me,
You killed me,
You fought me,

You cut me open,
Ripped out my organs,
I can't heal,
I can't repair,
Though do you care?

I have not died yet,
Seems as though you haven't got to my golden heart,
The still-beating one,
You can't get there,
Though if you did you would be killing me.

You're harvesting my blood for fuel,
My organs for resources,
Am I just here for you,

For you to rip me apart,
And then try to put your mess back together?

You have hurt me,
You have harvested me,
You have destroyed me,
I have had enough,
I have given up fighting for you.

Charlie Thomas (14)
Bruern Abbey Senior School, Chilton

The ADHD In Me

In the still of the night,
My thoughts are racing, they need erasing.
All I must do is use my pen,
Then the art of writing can begin.
My thoughts become silent,
It helps me hide from the feeling of violence,
That ADHD cause us to feel,
The smile on my face always seems real.

All they can see is a child who is lazy,
Naughty, obnoxious, untidy, and hazy.
My mind often wonders, I'm not really there,
They shout and scream, it's hard to bear.
"Where are your pens? Your book is not out?"
"Boy, are you lazy, I know this no doubt."
"Leave this class, You are a waste of space,"
"You don't mind, do you, that I'm right in your face?"

This is the way my brain works,
On constant overdrive with anxiety and it hurts
My teachers support me and help me succeed.

Kaiden Bolton (13)
Chiltern Way Academy, Prestwood

Missing The Other Half Of Me

I used to have hot water,
I used to have a working phone.
I used to have food on the table
And a place I could call home.
People try to avoid me,
They walk right out of my way.
I wish I could have a roof over my head
And a place that I could stay.

I'm more than happy to work for a living,
I will even sing or dance.
I just need that opportunity;
I just need that one chance.
I wish I could sail away from this place,
On my make-believe boat.
I wish I had a blanket or even a warm coat.
She was my best friend;
I was lucky enough to call her my wife.
Since the day that she left me,
I haven't had happiness in my life.

Alfie Hobbs (14)
Chiltern Way Academy, Prestwood

Mental Health

Every weekday I dread waking up to my alarm.
It's just my reminder that I'm stuck at a school
Full of people that don't care about me
I'm tired and drained all the time,
I just want to feel something different
But I go anyway and put a smile on my face
Like a show dog wanting to just make people proud for once.
Comment after comment about my appearance and the way I act
I hate them, what did I do to them?
"Why don't you just talk about it then, if it's that bad?"
I can't... I've tried.
I feel a painful knot in my throat that makes me want to cry
I don't want to cry, it makes me feel weak
So, I will write about it instead.

Freya Wakefield
Chiltern Way Academy, Prestwood

Autism In Me

A s a person with autism, can you relate?
U nderstood, different but not a mistake.
T ested daily with a change of routine
I just want autism to not be seen.
S ensitive, sweet and super intelligent
M istakes we might make when we feel inconvenient.

I nside the school, the home or outside,
N o one understands the never-ending ride.

M e and my autism go hand in hand,
E veryone needs to start to understand.

Harrison Osborne (13)
Chiltern Way Academy, Prestwood

The Fog Of ADHD

Looking through the fog of ADHD.
I'm so often misunderstood,
I would change in a heartbeat if I could.
Take my hand and listen to me,
I want to share a secret about ADHD.
I want you to know there is more to me,
I'm not defined by it, you see.
I'm sensitive, kind and lots of fun,
I could run with you and sit in the sun.
Looking through the fog of ADHD.

Ben Wilson (14)
Chiltern Way Academy, Prestwood

Through My Eyes

Through my old eyes
Like the Joker and Harley Quinn
You were my biggest sin.
Like Bonnie and Clyde
You were the one I guide
Toxic love
Even though I love you like a dove.
You were my high
Now I have to say goodbye.

Through my new eyes
I got so deep
I couldn't find my own feet.
Stuck in the crowds
Trying to get to the clouds.
Demons in my brain
Causing so much pain
Broken heart
Feeling like I got hit by a dart.

Daisy Soppelsa (17)
Clare Lodge, Glinton

In Our Eyes

In our eyes
You're saving lives
When someone dies
We start to cry.
When we're in pain
You're coming in the rain
When we are asleep
You're up to the beat
When mental health is loud
You're always around.

Darcie Taggart
Clare Lodge, Glinton

Shades Of A Struggle

In the nutshell of teenage dreams,
A life embellished with vibrant seams.
I take on the path as a minority,
In a love-hate world, a polarity.
A phantasmagoria of hues within,
Life holds the battles I begin.
In the glass, reflections collide,
A dance of recognition, side by side.
Love whispers, hate echoes,
An enigma within closed doors.
In the fusion of adolescent strife,
I navigate the decline and flow of life.
The world, a canvas of contradictions,
Bridges are built on fractured foundations.
In the garden of acceptance, seeds are sown,
Yet weeds of prejudice refuse to be overthrown.
Love blooms in clandestine corners,
Eyes that scrutinize, voices that jeer,
Yet resilience whispers in my ear.
Love, a stranger in the darkest night,
Ignites the flames of a struggle for life.
I paint my story in vibrant words,
Of being a teen, where love elicits.
Hate may linger, but love prevails.

Claire Olajide (14)
De Aston School, Market Rasen

Opposites

Life and death are opposites
But everyone knows that opposites attract
With yin there is yang and yang there is yin
Nobody knows why but there is
Something about hate that makes you love
And when that love is strong enough
You can do anything if you believe,
If you try you have more of a chance.
Life is just a placeholder
Whilst you wait for death's cold embrace
No one knows when it will be,
But you know how much your family will miss you,
How much they will cry
They will hurt, so whilst you read this
Remember, you are loved by everyone you know
They may not show it
If they take time out of their day to acknowledge you

Opposites attract.

Isabel Hernon (12)
De Aston School, Market Rasen

The Environment

Hidden away from everything
Emerald vines wrapping up tightly
As if it were a snake
Easing up ever so slightly

Hidden away from everything
Blankets of crinkly leaves
All oranges and greens
Flying as the wind breathes

Hidden away from everything
The sound of crickets echo
Beetles swarming
Lizards like geckos

Hidden away from everything
A bird's breath-taking melody
Brightly coloured birds gliding
It's pure beauty

Hidden away from us
A whole unseen universe
One filled with life
Where nature is so diverse.

Charlotte Perkins (12)
De Aston School, Market Rasen

Heroes

In shadows deep, where courage gleams,
Heroes rise with noble dreams.
Their hearts ablaze, a fearless spark,
Guiding light through the daunting dark.

Through trials fierce, they boldly tread,
A path that others fear to tread.
With strength that stems from deep within,
They conquer battles, virtue kin

A symphony of valour sung,
In deeds unsung, their praises rang.
With selfless hearts and hands held high
Heroes soar and touch the boundless sky.

In tales untold, their legacy weaves,
A tapestry of hope that never leaves.
For every hero, a chapter unfolds,
In the saga of courage, their story holds.

Ben Kennedy (14)
De Aston School, Market Rasen

When Cats Are Left Home

He's gone, hooray,
Now I can be on my way,
To my evil, mysterious plan,
It started with a man,
But it ends with a cat.

He's gone, hooray,
It's the perfect day,
I jump up onto the worktop,
With a graceful little hop,
Because I am a cat.

He's gone, hooray,
Time to really play,
With one elegant sweep,
And trying not to fall asleep,
I knock down a cookbook, like a cat.

He's home, oh no,
Time to now go,
It's been a blast,
And I'm glad you asked,
What do cats do when cats are left home?

Amelia Parker (12)
Etonbury Academy, Arlesey

The Day My World Collapsed

Fiery spittle shoots from the caged metal,
Waves lapping my shoes,
What more could I possibly lose?

Everyone's screaming, sprinting for survival,
Tears running down my face,
How could I keep this pace?

The power exerted which none of us wield,
Using each other as our humble shield.
The boats are ready,
Packed but steady.

My home I won't find again,
Humankind let me down again,
Constant suffering, from the fury of the men.

I will always remember this as the day I tried to flee,
I will never again set foot on the sea.

Hannah Olkes (14)
Etonbury Academy, Arlesey

Shawn Mendes Poem

Shawn Mendes stitches,
Always give me itches,
It brightens up my day,
What can I say,
It's the greatest in town,
It takes the crown.

Mercy though,
I know,
It's second best,
I am blessed.

Treat you better,
Is like a letter,
It's always great,
And better with a mate.

There's nothing holding me back,
The longest of the pack,
It's pretty good,
Although misunderstood.

Shawn Mendes,
He's the best singer,
He's the winner,
Best singer forever.

Charlotte Jarvis (11)
Etonbury Academy, Arlesey

It's Sunny And It's Raining

It's sunny, it's bright
There's not a cloud in the sky
You can't convince me that
There are people that cry
There's joy and mirth
Love and light
So don't tell me that there's
Pain
Because there is only
Peace
There is no
Suffering
Because really there is
Perfection
There's love
So why do you even say that
It's all gone dark
It's raining, it's pouring

(now read from the bottom up)

Ella Greaney (14)
Etonbury Academy, Arlesey

What Is Love?

When someone dies you feel heartbroken
But the love is never fake
The families will miss you
But there is someone new
Love is real
They will always make you kneel
When you miss them
For real
But they are always in your heart.
They will play always the harp.
They are gone but they are shown.
This is the end.
They will be always your friend.

Mateusz Iwanicki (11)
Horbury Academy, Horbury

Swapping Lives

In a twist of fate, our paths entwined,
I wake up in a world not mine.
A famous face, a life of glamour,
A world of stardom, bright and sparkling.

But as I walk in these famous shoes,
I feel the weight of public views.
The cameras flash, a life in the spotlight, no time for rest.

The world expects a spectacular show.
Yet in my heart, the real me knows.
A celebrity life, a glittering appearance.
Underneath it all a soul unscarred.

As I long for the life I left behind,
I see the human in the celebrity's mind.
Pleading for sanity a quiet retreat,
A chance to live, not just to compete.

So as we swap these lives, you and I.
We learn the truth beyond the sky.
No life is perfect, no matter the face,
We're all just souls in the human race.

Michelle Evboifo (12)
International Community School London, Paddington

I Am Mandy Fabian

I am the eagle, proud and free,
A smart dolphin, racing into the sea.

Caring for children, both of them strong,
While travelling the world, bringing them along.

Although I want to keep them in my nest, I have to let them leave,
Because I know they will be alright, I won't have to grieve.

Inside my nest, there is another,
He says he loves me because I am a good mother.

As I am developing short films, stage plays, and more,
I have made my very first movie and I am hoping it soars!

Adventuring places I haven't seen before,
Though while I am there, people say I will never make a score.

No matter the hate, no matter the size,
I know I will be safe, as I start to rise.

Delilah Fabian (11)
International Community School London, Paddington

I Am Billie Eillish

I walk like a panther
I talk like nobody's there when you stare
I feel scared of the flashing lights
They just don't stop flashing
It's not fair
People are saying I'm sad
But if you were me you would understand
I am like a monkey in a cage
Singing is my saviour
If I do not write they will despise me
But they all care about what I do
Not who I am
When I want to be a human
The lions come and stop me
From connecting to life they roar
I roar back and I know you're copying me
Like my reflection in the mirror
Do you really want to be me now?

Connie Corfield
International Community School London, Paddington

I Am Ariana Grande

I am a lioness strong and free,
The voice of an angel, can't you see?
Day to day, time to time,
I have no time, no time to rhyme.
I am a colouring book without the pages,
The broken heart that sometimes rages.
Goodbye to the sunshine, hello to the rain,
From unicorns and rainbows to constant pain.
Cameras are everywhere, I'm the disguise,
It's hard to be famous, you do realise?

Melania Hamrick (11)
International Community School London, Paddington

The Kitsune Of The Forest

Among the great trees of pine, a creature resides,
Moss-green tipped paws across the ground glide.
Four verdant tails swishing in the dappled light,
Large tufted ears, and azure eyes bright.
Jade-like swirls glow across a sleek body almost white;

A forest Kitsune, padding through the night.

It turns, scanning the woods around,
Ears pricked for the slightest sound.
A pine marten here, snuffling the ground.
A deer herd stood atop a mound.
A lynx, tawny coat brushing an ash,
By a brook, a kingfisher's blue-orange flash.

And then... a nearby crash.
A sapling falls, its branches spread,
Accompanied by a heavy tread.
Lumberjacks, from whom animals fled.

The creatures around cowered in fear,
From lynx to pine marten, kingfisher to deer.
They came to plunder and ravage the wood.
But in their way, the Kitsune stood.

As it bolted forward it uttered a call to war,
A fiercely wild howl that rose to a roar.
The lumberjacks leered, their feet planted wide,

But more animals came, tide upon tide.
Fur and scale, claw and feather,
They came side by side, all nature together.

It was then the lumberjacks realised their mistake,
Away they ran, making the pine branches shake.
From then they treated the forest with care,
And the story of the Kitsune they did scarcely share
But if you allow nature to grow as it should,
Then you might glimpse a grateful Kitsune in the depths of a wood.

Cari Hicks (12)
Islwyn High School, Oakdale

3045

I see the future,
Metallic flying cars
Life on Mars
Buildings peaking high
Puffy clouds drifting by
Beaming city lights
Amazing sights

I see the future,
Awesome AI
A nice blue sky
Intelligent robots
Burning hot
Beautiful is it not?

Rohan Lewis (12)
Islwyn High School, Oakdale

I Remember

I remember the day I came home, small and scared.
I was welcomed with boxes of toys and a comfy bed,
And lots of cuddles too!

I remember lots of walks at the beach,
The sand covering my paws
And my humans chasing me
When it was time to go home,
I remember begging for food
During their dinner time
And licking the plates clean
After they were done.

I remember cuddling them when they cried,
But this time it is different.
As I lie here on a cold bed,
In a weird-smelling room,
Surrounded by my family that loves me.

Lauren Murray (16)
Milne's High School, Fochabers

Sick Day

My mind is pulsing from the headache that slurs my brain
Into the soup that Mum makes when I am sick.
I pick it apart like the bread and season it with a sickened stomach.
Mum's offerings: swirls of cream, garnished with green,
Even though my mouth tastes of breakfast that's in
the toilet.
I have no appetite.
Later, when I am back at school and the attention is away from my mind,
Starved, it begs for the little attention it is given.
A faulty machine, computing the wish of a future
Where being sick isn't the only day I get her,
Where I can rest in the arms of my mother
Without a thermometer in my mouth and sweat above
my lip.
A safe place that smells like weekday dinners and
clean washing,
Like all the other little girls my age.
Their minds process only luxuries they take for granted,
While I savour the creamy bitterness of what I can gulp.
I copy their smiles and the crumbs of their conversations in
the playground
Before, exhausted, I go back to my bench.
I don't know how to nourish myself.

Lily Bertram (15)
New River College Medical, London

Through The Eyes Of Orpheus

Thud! Thud! Thud!
Orpheus couldn't tell if the sound was his feet
As he trudged up the cavernous tunnel,
Or his anxious heart pumping away inside his chest.

He had his eyes trained on the light before him.
He could not dare to move them away
From that spot for a second,
Even when the bright sun blinded his vision.

Thud! Thud! Thud!
He strained his ears... was it her?
His dearest Eurydice would be behind him now.

He ached to look back at her,
But instead, he focused on what he hoped
Was the sound of her feet tapping
Along the stone path, just as his were.

His beautiful Eurydice,
He couldn't bear the thought of living without her.
That was the desperation that drew him
To accept the king of the underworld's challenge:

"Walk to the overworld and she will follow
But not once look back at your beloved,
Lest she be lost forever."

The gods were fickle ones,
They so liked to play with mortals such as them.
Was Hades using them for his own entertainment?
Was it a trick?

Dark clouded Orpheus's vision.
He closed his eyes to avoid looking back
And he began humming a low tune:

Hmm, hmm, hmm

Perhaps he was a fool to trust a god,
Perhaps the lord of death
Had Eurydice trapped in his kingdom now
As Orpheus walked further and further away from her.

Hmm, hmm, hmm

He raised his voice so as to drown out
The doubtful thoughts plaguing in his mind.
Was that the sound of Eurydice's feet or his own?
Was her heart beating in tandem with his
Or would it never beat again?

Hmm, hmm, hmm

The sound became shaky in his throat
As he struggled to continue his song.
His muse, forever his source of inspiration,
His beloved Eurydice,

He could almost feel her absence,
Her abandonment.

Orpheus became frenzied;
Sounds surrounded him
Drowning out his unsure song,
As with one fatal turn, he looked back,

There she was.
Eurydice clutched her chest
And her eyes filled with despair and shock.
He reached out to her
But his hands touched nothing.
She was gone.
He knelt on the ground.

Tap! Tap! Tap!

The sounds of Orpheus's tears
Bouncing off the stone floor.

Erin Young (17)
R.E.A.L Education, Mansfield

In The Eyes Of The Moon

As night hits I sit down and stare at the moon.
I don't know why but it helps when I feel blue.
In this world, it's hard to find someone
Who genuinely relates to you.
Although I see myself
When I look in the eyes of the moon.

In the eyes of the moon,
I can't help but feel gloom.
When I look around,
I see the company are way different to me.
The stars all shine their own light,
Fitting in with every right.
While I, out of all my company,
Why, why is it only me?

In the eyes of the moon,
I battle against my own fume.
Although, as I go through this
And when I start to feel helpless.
An unexpected visit gets paid by the sun.

The sun understands me
But I still can't help but feel jealous.
As she shines her rays effortlessly
And gets a crowd who stares enjoyably.
She knows how to play her role,

She's everything I can't get under control.
Yet, as much as I despise her achievement,
I can't help but love her amendment.

As the sun finishes her play,
And her audience has gone away.
The sun gives me her light,
To use it during the night.
I go out and shine, showing off my talent
When the clock hits nine.
A talent undiscovered,
That my quiet self keeps covered.

I enter the stage and show my spark,
When all the audience's chairs are out of work.
From backstage, I finally get to show myself onstage.
Well again, that's when no one is watching, of course.

However what if I say,
That what the moon thinks is wrong.
As she is unaware of the presence that stays unknown.
The presence of a tired human,
Who stays up watching the moon
Shining light into her room,
During that time she hides away
And is only able to think of how she sees herself
In the eyes of the moon.

Aliyyah (13)
Royal Greenwich Trust School, Greenwich

Social Anxiety

I walk through the school halls
And feel their eyes on me
But that's even if they are,
I mean...
Why
Would
Anyone
Look
At me?

I wonder if I talk too loud or too much
Or laugh too hard, even the way I walk bothers me

I tell others about the way I feel
And they say that 'it's all in my head'
And that 'they feel stressed too'
And I immediately feel worried for them
And I forget my worries as if they never existed.

Guilt eats me up inside and digs my heart out.
Why did I have to talk about myself right now?
What's wrong with me?
I feel suffocated and remind myself to breathe *inhale* *exhale*
I've got a huge smile on my face
But on the inside, I feel a disgrace

It was terrible, like waking up from a nightmare
But realising you aren't awake at all

Are they talking about me down the hall?
Impossible, they don't even know me
Am I annoying?
All I did was pick up a pen for someone
I have to keep up a front, a guard all day
But it gets exhausting
I'm tired, why can't I be free
Like everyone else?

It enveloped me in a constant state of gloom
My dreams were withering and I was in agony.
Day after day, anxiety spun its web around my thoughts
And spread to all corners of my heart.

Hatred
Hatred for myself.
Pathetic.
That's what they must be
Whispering about.
I sure am pathetic.
I realise that now that it's not their fault.
It's mine.
I lack responsibility and sense.

Destiny Njoku (12)
Royal Greenwich Trust School, Greenwich

My Thoughts...

In the drawer, forgotten, I reside,
A pen with tales to confide.
Ink flows through my slender veins,
Capturing thoughts like falling rain.

Oh, the pages I've adorned with prose,
Witness to triumphs and heartfelt woes.
From love letters to dreams untold,
I'm a vessel of stories, a pen of old.

Amidst the clutter on the dusty shelf,
A forgotten book sighs to itself.
Each page is a journey, a world to explore,
I yearn for eager hands, forevermore.

A clock on the wall ticks away,
Measuring time in a rhythmic sway.
In each tick, a moment's fleeting grace,
Yet, I'm stuck in this predictable space.

A lonely chair by the fireside,
Remembering the warmth of a friend by its side.
Now a silent witness to passing days,
Hoping for laughter that forever stays.

Inanimate, yet not devoid of thought,
Every object's tale is silently sought.

Through quiet moments, we come alive,
In the stories woven, we all survive.

Samira Yakubu (12)
Royal Greenwich Trust School, Greenwich

The Hourglass

In the shadows of the schoolyard, she stands alone,
A target for the cruel words, a heart made of stone.
They mock her clothes, her hair, her every stride,
Her spirit wilting, wounded deep inside.

She bears their taunts with a silent, heavy heart,
Each cutting remark tearing her apart.
She longs for solace in a world so unkind,
But the echoes of their laughter haunt her mind.

Yet in the darkness, a flicker of hope remains,
A strength within her that no torment can chain.
She finds her voice, speaking out against the pain,
Drawing courage from the tears that fall like rain.

For she is more than the labels they impose,
Her worth was not defined by their jeers that arose.
With resilience as her armour, she stands tall,
A beacon of light in a world where bullies crawl.

So let us stand with her, against the tide,
Lending our support, standing by her side.
For in unity and kindness, we forge a space,
Where the bullied finds a loving embrace.

Chisom Elemide (13)
Royal Greenwich Trust School, Greenwich

Down, Down, Down

Explosions all around me
Fighter jets are dropping like flies.
The enemies are getting forever closer
The roar of their engines.
My heart beats faster every second.
A blinding flash of light.
I'm going down, down, down.
The ground pulls my jet down, down, down.
An invisible force holding me back, pulling me back.
The ground is getting forever closer.
My hand reaches out.
I press down on the escape button.
My eyes close.
I breathed in.
I opened them.
A smile lit up my face.
I was no longer going down, down, down.

Neave Foster (11)
Royal Greenwich Trust School, Greenwich

Stop Hiding

In an unknown place, I stay quiet and still.
Forged into war, more vicious than ever.
A great war between two powerful nations.
We are tired.
No matter how hard, brutal and powerful you are,
we still stand.
But what caused you to do this?
What caused you to take thousands of lives away
from families?
What caused you to burn, wreck and invade our
community?
We have been oppressed since 1967, when will you stop?
Our holy land is coming down in pieces.
Please, please take a stand for Palestine.

Tofunmi Ayeni (12)
Royal Greenwich Trust School, Greenwich

Refugee's Eyes

The grey skies in his eyes,
Are a disguise to hide the sunshine that lies,
Behind the lining of his skin,
And that's only the beginning of him;
Everything that's ever lived
Migrates through his veins.
Fire rages inside his rib cage
So they must escape to find safety.
I've made some space inside of me
In case he needs a place to hide the refugees.

Sonela Seferi (13)
Royal Greenwich Trust School, Greenwich

My Aunt Is Strong And My Sister Is Strong

My aunt is stronger than she thinks
But to me, she is stronger
She has different things wrong with her
She is strong and she thinks she gives up quickly
But to me, she never gives up
My sister is strong
But to her, she is not strong
To me, she will always be there for me
Thank you for listening to my story
Make sure to never give up, okay?

Grace Igglesden (11)
Royal Greenwich Trust School, Greenwich

Who Inspires Me The Most

The people who inspire me are my parents
Because they work very hard
I want to be like them
That is one thing
And the second thing is
They help me with my homework
And the third thing is that they have amazing jobs
My dad is a gunman and my mom is a private nursery worker
I love both jobs but I don't know which one to choose.

Kristi Igglesden (11)
Royal Greenwich Trust School, Greenwich

Believe

Believe in yourself
And the power within
Become your master
And be your best friend

Believe in power
You have deep inside
Behold inner peace
And in wisdom

Believe in your heart
Every word that you say
Be yourself in every way
Be trusting in God
And let faith lead the way.

Fadesewa Afeni (12)
Royal Greenwich Trust School, Greenwich

The Empty Bucket

I'm not empty or hollow,
I am filled only with the historical whispers of the sand.
My colours are always bright and seeable,
But I'm always left behind.
You separate me from my only friend,
And leave it covered in the golden bed.
You abandon me,
Something so simple but so commonly overlooked.
You give me hope then let me wash away in the sea
of salty tears.
Why am I punished due to your lack of love and empathy?
Now I am left to float endlessly in the water of your
neglection.
I am made to bring memories and smiles
But you have broken my significance in this world...
How long until my name is non-existent?
You left me?
Why do you always leave me?

Felicity-Jo Thornton (15)
Sharples School, Bolton

Her Eyes

Sure her eyes may be dull and lifeless
Her cold glare frightened others
Others who don't care to look under her dead eyes
Because if they did, if they did care to look behind her eyes
They would notice a small girl
A small girl whose eyes glisten with life and hope
And this small girl will tell you stories of her life
Of how she conquered some of the hardest obstacles
But not once did her toothy grin fade
Slowly but surely you start to realise
Realise why the girl with the lifeless eyes
Is so cruel to outsiders
She's just protecting the girl inside her
From any more harm.

Muzen Shenaif (16)
Sharples School, Bolton

The Eye

The land began to freeze
My eyes began to water
I noticed a big eye
In the corner of my eye

In the eye was
Ladies dancing
People singing
All but one person
The guy with a giant eye
But that was my dream

I woke up
I saw the eye
All but pain
As I looked in the eye
The future came
Tragedy struck
I started shaking continuously
I froze

The world unfrozen
As I was frozen, I looked in the eye once again
And time went back
And back
And back
Till there was no earth to be seen.

Aqsa Alli (11)
Sharples School, Bolton

Creations

Every day he approached the easel
Barbed in thick brush paint on his pale apron
Hands red, skin stiff against the handle
Each day he painted a new world

Either dressed in darkness, dawn or dying light
Pastel moons or watercoloured suns flame the landscape white
Developing scene after scene
With gardens and rivers the space between
Acrylic mountains
But absent from his masterpieces was flesh
Blood and beating life
That validated his colours and starlit skies
So with finer care and a gentle rhythm, she was fashioned

Her smile was cut burgundy with quick strokes
That greased her lips with purpose
And she soon began to breathe
She felt the air sobering her face in the carving breeze
She smelt the grass, the itching scent of summer
Meld with hints of willow and water
She fell to love, to the obligation for the beauty around her

And then she felt sunlight
And as the light slipped past her shoulders
It gathered behind her

Pooling into shadow that bound to her back
Each day he gave her light
Sold her streams and brought her forests
And all the light did not matter
For all she cast was darkness.

Patrick Gambles (17)
St Anselm's College, Prenton

Say No!

Alcohol isn't good for your body,
It affects your heart and liver,
Think twice about having a drink;
Imagine all those toxins
Flowing through your blood like a river;
It's easy, just to say no!

Peer pressure rains down on you like a storm,
Like a tornado stalking you,
The pressure will haunt you, putting you in bad form;
It will never leave you alone unless you say no!

Sometimes it's difficult when you're having fun,
All you want to do is have a little sip,
So it can be tempting to just have one,
But don't let your emotions dip;
All you have to do is say no!

Leona Belo
St Patrick's College, Dungannon

My Beloved Country

E ast Timor is as warm as an oven,
A nd the waves and sea love tickling the shore,
S ometimes I miss my beloved country,
T he country seems to be calling my name

T oday or tomorrow, I will never be ashamed of my ethnicity,
I wish more people would recognise East Timor,
M any, many more visiting and talking about my country,
O h, how I envy the people there right now,
R adiant sunshine gleaming through your window...

This is East Timor!

Ana Maria Baptista Amaral
St Patrick's College, Dungannon

World's Strongest Man

He can deadlift like an elephant,
He is as tall as a giraffe,
He is a beast admired by all
Who is he?

Answer: Eddie Hall!

Teagan Gildernew
St Patrick's College, Dungannon

Refugees

A slaughter ground for hearts,
Over one thousand beats killed within a few seconds,
I had to travel somewhere
As they demolished my childhood in front of my eyes.
Buses, cars and planes,
Minutes, hours and days,
Just to get to a place that I couldn't even call home.
I held on tight to those I was familiar with,
Trying not to get lost in crowds.
I held on tight to my few belongings,
Because I couldn't simply settle down.
People looked at me differently,
As though I wasn't accepted,
To them, I was a waste of space, an alien in despair.
It felt like someone was stabbing me billions of times over.
The loneliness of it all,
The dirty looks and snarky comments
About my race and religion,
I wanted my mum and dad,
But we both know I can't get them back.

Amelie Loveday (14)
The Petersfield School, Petersfield

Silent And Discrete

Average day situating myself on a seat,
Trying my best to become silent and discrete,
The muffled murmuring of a man once again,
The revving of a vessel takes off with their yen.

Echos of my past beating in my head,
The memories of torture come back while in my bed,
The feeling of pain haunts me in my dreams,
As I hear the constant horror of neighbouring screams.

One by one, the silence grows,
Taken to a place that nobody knows,
Each day the revving of the beast becomes more deafening,
As I await the harsh reality of the reckoning.

The final building opposite me,
There lay a family of three,
In that direction, they are very near,
Then they are shoved into the machine's rear.

One after another my neighbours disappeared,
Stolen by the group that's feared,
As I sit in petrification and shock,
My door receives a violent harsh knock.

The final bang of a gun is heard,
And then my vision begins to blur,

A red coat is all I'm wearing,
All to be heard is shattered swearing

The road ahead is trying their best to be silent and discrete,
Unfortunately, death is all they'll meet.

James Landrum-Patton (14)
The Petersfield School, Petersfield

The Sentinel

Another shot, another crater in my skin.
They are here, that I know.
They are afraid, this I will make sure of.

They think that their musket shots will hurt me.
But now we both know that they don't stand a chance.
They might not understand why they are going to die.
But I know their crime, as do my creators.

They are trespassers on the grounds of this burial site.
They are the trespassers and I am the guardian.
They are wrong and I am right.

Another crack in my stone skin
And another musket shot is used.
Another rake of iron claws
And the trespasser is dead,
Musket lying useless by his side.

They believe themselves to be explorers.
I believe them to be murderers.
Murderers took the lives of the tribe,
Forcing them on the road before the migration of
the buffalo.

And now they want the burial ground.
I have watched them silently for years now,
Building their homes on their stolen land.

And now they want the burial ground.
My burial ground.

I can hear their musket shots in the distance.
They are here, I know it.
They are scared, this I am sure of.

Josh Marchant (14)
The Petersfield School, Petersfield

I Promise That I'm Trying

I'm a teenage boy, not a robot,
I'm just trying to make you proud.
You don't understand; I can't make a sound.
No peace, just an unsolved puzzle piece,
Tears are burning, fears are churning,
Don't you understand? I'm not learning.
This feeling: is it concerning?
Thoughts? Worries? So many, too many…
No one has noticed the mask; it's working
Don't you understand? This *is* me trying.

They told me that I'd wasted all my potential,
That the cages I am trapped in are mental.
Keep the feeling in, I won't shout them out,
Everyone here seems to have their doubts
About me.
And what I could make up to be.
It's a never-ending cycle,
With my truest and biggest rival,
Being the boy that they all see,
But for one, I disagree.

I attend my school every day,
Just ignore what they all will say.
My smile is slowly fading,
Their comments are so degrading.
Keep up with the act,

Never react.
And maybe, just maybe
They will understand,
This *is* me trying.

Rubie McIntyre-Lamek (13) & Charlotte
The Petersfield School, Petersfield

Toxic

I am trapped.
A prisoner to him.
The way he doesn't care for me.
That's not how it's supposed to be.
I am a bird in a cage.
Just for show,
But behind the scenes,
He's verbally abusing me.

I am lonely.
He cut off all my friends.
My family.
All I have is the cold, hateful feeling of darkness.
And the bitterness of his rejection.

I am scared.
The awful way he treats me.
Beats me.
Makes me feel worthless, see?
He uses me.
Harms me.
All to make himself happy.
About himself.
If I fight I'll be found,
And hurt twice as much as before.
Is there no way for me?
Is this my fault?

What did I do wrong?
I'm sorry!
This endless cycle will just go on.
And I'm not strong enough to stop the wheel,
And step away free.
I am trapped.
I am trapped.
I can't get out.

Mika Valdivia a l'Onions (14)
The Petersfield School, Petersfield

When You Think Of Me

Do you remember my face?
Do you remember that night?
You're the one to blame
You will be now and forever more

Let your guilt overcome you,
Let it fill you or kill you
Let yourself take the blame,
Let it pile up upon you

You're the monster I was warned of
The one who made me watch my back
Yet I let you into my life
And you took advantage of that

I don't think any of those thoughts
I never would towards you
You were no monster or threat
You think you are but no

Your mind wanted closure
That's when you didn't get
You became the target
No one blamed you for my death

You don't believe those around
Who tells you that you're free

Your mind is chained
Entrapped, restrained
As you think of me.

Kayleigh Skipp (14)
The Petersfield School, Petersfield

It All Stops Now

It all stops now,
Scared to come to school,
Making up excuses,
Why is everyone so cruel?
Coming home with bruises,

It all stops now,
Shaking with fear
Shouting, "Leave me alone!"
This is all I hear
I'm practically unknown.

It all stops now,
Alone every single day
When will it stop
I wish it would all just go away
It's all just non-stop.

It all stops now.
Hiding away,
Scared for myself,
Wonder what will happen today,
All they think about is themselves.

It all stops now,
Walking to school,
Will it be a good day?

This only happens in school,
Let me off today.

It all stops now,
Everyday banging on,
Hitting me with all the cruel words,
I wish it could be gone,
All I hear are the birds.

James Kentish (14)
The Petersfield School, Petersfield

Stop!

Since the beginning of human beings
Starting with Adam and Eve,
You took away my evergreen
And had nothing to say, not in the slightest,
What about my thoughts and feelings?
Now I'm going to hold my head high
And say, the world is *mine!*

Stop!

I was made for love and to flourish
I was there at your service,
But all you did was cut me down,
Like one of my precious ever-growing trees
I heard my trees cry
And there was nothing I could do!

Stop!

Stop all the:
Deforestation
Overpopulation
Overfishing
Fossil fuels
Plastic

Stop!

Why did I ever keep spinning?
Why did I just spin in silence?
Why did I never stop you?

So here is my final plea

Stop!

Joe Tully (14)
The Petersfield School, Petersfield

The Life Of Seeing Everything Every Day

Being a cloud is a difficult thing;
You never get any rest,
And you're always watching everything
That's going on in the world.
It could be good or bad;
You will never know what will happen.
It's always a surprise, but sometimes, not a good surprise.
When you're a cloud, you can see all the conflicts,
And you can see all the ways people are making the world a bad place.
There are barely any positives of being a cloud,
Except for the good views.
It does get very boring, seeing the same thing day after day
After the world has done its full rotation.
It's sometimes dark, depending on where I am.
I wish I wasn't a cloud so I could run around and have fun,
Rather than feeling upset so often
About what's happening in the world.

Nia Lovat Pugh (13)
The Petersfield School, Petersfield

My Party

Music and people are all I heard,
All my words came out kind of slurred.
I saw someone, dressed in all pink.
I told them, "Do me a favour, hold my drink."
They looked nice enough, I thought I could trust them
I didn't really care though;
My throat was already filling with phlegm.

I stumbled to the toilet
This was one of my favourite bits
Talking to all the girls in there
And comforting the ones in despair

I come back, grab my drink once again
Downed it all and realised it was half past 10
I started feeling woozy
Something wasn't right

My drink?
What did they do to it?
Why didn't I stop and think?
Me getting sick, what is their benefit?

Izzy Oleary (14)
The Petersfield School, Petersfield

Death Row

I feel sympathy,
Sympathy for those who go through it.
I am one of those,

Rows full of pain
Rows full of depression,
Imprisoned within bodies

I feel locked in, forever in a lockdown
I'm trapped, shouting left and right
All the haunting thoughts
Will be over soon enough

I walk down a long corridor
It's like a walk of shame.
As if I've been caught, caught up with the past
20 long years and this is where it ends.

Silence, the silence is loud,
Witnesses look like a one-of-a-kind,

I sat waiting
I couldn't see anything
The crowd held on tight to chairs
Silence
Not a word left.

Ronnie Bradley (14)
The Petersfield School, Petersfield

Child Of Hate

I am a child of discrimination
You call me slurs and yell hate
You pressure me to change for your satisfaction
You act as if I am less than human
You can't stand being near me
I am a person

I am a victim of prejudice
I get excluded and mocked
I get attacked for you to feel better
I get laughed at
I am human

Under all that
You and I aren't so different
I go to school
I dream
I love
I have friends and family

But you don't see me that way
You are blinded by hate
You see what people tell you to see
If you opened your eyes
You would see
That I am human.

Willow Perring (14)
The Petersfield School, Petersfield

Match Day

Big game today, the final of the cup,
Good chance of winning, if we don't mess up,
To achieve this dream,
We must work as a team.

As the game starts,
The fans begin to chant,
And now fear rises upon me,
I realise I need to believe.

The full-time whistle blows,
And the game had no goals,
The game goes to a penalty shootout,
I start to panic and doubt.

It's my turn to shoot,
And I tie up my boot,
I kick the ball,
And... goal!

The team celebrates,
The opposition felt nothing but devastate,
And although fear filled my inner,
After all, we were the winners!

Frankie Ruffle (14)
The Petersfield School, Petersfield

The Forgotten War

The guns are banging
And rifles are clanging,
Whilst conflict's raging
With the sun blazing

It's the Gulf War,
The planes roar
Whilst the Iraqi snore,
In the Gulf War.

The many times they went back
They fixed as much as a little crack
Many were ordered to stay
In a FOB, that's where stuff took place.

Saddam Hussein
Invading Kuwait,
Was it really worthy
Of your own fate?

The coalition won this war,
And I'm sure we'll win many more.

Amidst the fighting
Lives were lost
Lest not forget
Those who were lost.

Harrison Granton (13)
The Petersfield School, Petersfield

"Incredible Things Can Happen" Marcus Rashford

"My dead nan could have scored that!"
"Your face makes me feel so sick"
"How can you live with that skin?"

This is my everyday,
People hating on me.
Sending vile threats over,
A solitary penalty.

I've fed hungry children,
Represented single mums.
Fought for fairness,
For each and every one.

I put a foot wrong,
Got the wrong result.
Waking up the next day,
Scrolling through insults.

Think of what you're saying,
The mud that you sling.
Your words have power,
Hate can change everything.

Delilah Carr (13)
The Petersfield School, Petersfield

Love Is Weakness

L ove is weakness, love is kindness,
O h, childish thoughts oh childish things,
V ery foolish, very sweet,
E ven if we are to learn,

I n the end, we will all crash and burn.
S ilence falls and silence will break

W ill I ever reawake?
E verything still, according to plan
A las, he is just a pawn in my hand
K eep believing my deceitful lies
N o escape, no matter how much he tries
E ven if he does begin to see
S how him lies, show him hate
S o that fool will come my way.

Reuben James (14)
The Petersfield School, Petersfield

Climate Change

I'm getting too hot,
That sun is taking over,
Soon, no more holidays on a yacht,
Something needs to change,

The monsters don't listen,
Buying new fancy cars,
That glisten,
Something needs to change,

There's not going to be another generation,
To make the switch,
To this nation,
Something needs to change,

Nobody understands,
What they are really doing,
They need a hand,
Something needs to change,

They're in too deep,
No fixing it now,
They're too weak,
Something needs to change.

Darcey Tebbutt (13)
The Petersfield School, Petersfield

The Mirror Never Lies

I used to think the mirror never lied
But I used to think a lot of things
So, putting that aside,

Mirror, mirror, on the wall,
Who's the fairest of them all?
It can't be me, I'll guarantee.
That much I can recall.

I'll steal the apple from Snow White.
For she doesn't *need* a valiant knight
And tell her what the mirror told me
She doesn't have to be the prettiest
Just to be seen.

I used to think the mirror never lied
But maybe I was wrong
Maybe it just couldn't decide.

Ellie Barnett (13)
The Petersfield School, Petersfield

From Heaven To Hell

Another day, another day in paradise.
Or at least, it was my paradise.
Running through cornfields,
Dancing with daisies.
Running so fast that no one could catch me

My owners couldn't catch me,
All I could be is happy
For all the money in the world,
Would never pay for another day in paradise.

Heaven and hell in so many ways,
Are very different but also the same
Running and jumping then... stop.
Wait a minute, where have they gone?

My owners and my friends
Where have they gone?
Now I stand alone.

Maryam Jones (13)
The Petersfield School, Petersfield

Marmite: A Questionable Decision

In the jar, I ponder, thick and bold,
A spread of intrigue, my thoughts unfold.
With a taste that differs, neither like nor despise,
A flavour journey, where uncertainty lies.

Spread me lightly, or heap me high,
On toast or crackers, I wonder why.
A taste sensation, a puzzle to solve,
A mysterious puzzle, a questionable taste.

Some moments I savour, others I hate,
In this jar of Marmite, my feelings are unknown.
For in this moment, I find a quest,
A taste adventure, at its best.

(Now read it from the bottom to the top.)

Ryan Chiverton (13)
The Petersfield School, Petersfield

Refugee

I stare into the distance
My eyes develop a glassy sheen
I think *do people really know of my existence*
Am I relevant
Am I seen?

I look out ahead
The crystal-clear waves are elegant
Dancing through the moonlit sky.

My mother next to me
The same sheen to her eye
Reflected in them is the sea.

I am a refugee
I am stranded
Come rescue me.
However, it's been commanded
You are not to assist
You are to abandon
A refugee like me.

Maisie Taylor (14)
The Petersfield School, Petersfield

Summer

S unny weather for 3 whole months
U nder the shade, living life like a deluxe
M idday at the lake, bake some cake and feed it to the ducks
M agical times, making memories, let's pick some fruit off the lemon trees
E ating ice creams all day long, you can never be wrong
R elaxing all week, hear the birds squeak, everyone is unique!

Rose Pinnick (13)
The Petersfield School, Petersfield

Shadowed Secrets

Whispers in the shadowed night,
Two hearts veiled from the light,
A love that dares not speak its name,
Yet burns with an unquenchable flame.

In the realm of secrets our love resides,
A clandestine dance where passion hides,
Bound by chains of circumstances and fate,
Yet our hearts dare to defy and create

Like two stars that burn in the night sky,
Our love shines bright though we must deny,
Aching hearts, longing to be free,
Yet bound by love that cannot be.

Evelyn Macdonald (13)
The Petersfield School, Petersfield

The Hand That Always Wants

You think that you're immune
That you can start your life brand new
You try to hide
Forever deny
But he'll always find you
That 'you are mine'
Until you die

Slicing through the mirrored sea
Jaws of death approaching me
I freeze in terror
But watch in awe
As it flips a fish into its jaw
There's pure innocence
In every promise you keep
And I know you feel everything so deep
It's the hand that always wants.

Ella Cooper (14)
The Petersfield School, Petersfield

Thud! Thud! Thud!

Smoke floods the floor and soon emerges us.
We aim
Wait
Crack a gunshot
A frightening thump as a body hits the ground
Thick red blood covers my boot

A figure emerges from the smoke, running
I shoot
A body drops dead.
He was dead
I drop my gun in shock
Disbelief came over me
I killed a man
Slash!
A knife pierces my body
Thud!

Blood covered my face
Thud after thud, we all dropped
Dead.

Oliver Wedley (13)
The Petersfield School, Petersfield

Drunk Drive

That one phone call killed me
Every word chipped my heart
He's crashed into a death tree
That night I wished we had never part
What if I never gave him a drink
Could I have stopped what happened that night
What would his family think
My thoughts flooded with fright
This was all my fault
My best friend coldly lay dead
He drove drunk like a lightning bolt
What if he had just gone to bed
I wasn't there, how is this fair?

Adriannah (13)
The Petersfield School, Petersfield

Prey

I want to be free,
Away from instability.
Poachers coach us,
To be scared.

Run, gallop, sprint.
I've lost so much.
Bang!
The sound of the gunshots.

I try to hide,
I can't.
I try to run,
I can't.

Sharp pain in my leg,
I fall down.
I try to get up,
I can't.

It's all over,
I *was* the predator,
But *now* I'm the prey.

Megan Bibb (14)
The Petersfield School, Petersfield

Being A Teenager

Today being a teenager is like a poisonous snake
And social media is its poison
A snake can't be trusted and its poison hurts everyone
And if you have been bitten, you can't get rid of it now
It's poison hurts but doesn't kill you but just until it hurts you more
It doesn't think it's enough to hurt you once so it wants more.

Karla Miu (14)
The Petersfield School, Petersfield

Through The Eyes Of A War Horse

The constant banging of firearms frightened me.
People falling to the ground, unconscious.
The harness around my neck bruised me.
The world surrounding me was set ablaze.

The shouting of men deafened me.
People running for their lives, exhausted.
The thought of death terrified me.
Would I ever be free again?

Lola Payne (14)
The Petersfield School, Petersfield

Dolor

For my love is a gift,
For your love is a treasure
For my time is a few pennies,
For your time is priceless
For my heart is broken,
For your heart is spared
For my life is worthless,
For your life has just begun
Forever my dear, you are now in peace.

Joshua Huffer (14)
The Petersfield School, Petersfield

At War

Streaks of bullets fly through the air
Thumps of lifeless bodies echoed in the silence
I sit curled in the trench
Gripping my head
Fathers, sons, nephews, grandsons
Begging for their lives
At the mercy of these horrible men.

Mia Humphries (14)
The Petersfield School, Petersfield

Wind Of Change

I am the wind, a force to be reckoned
A symphony of movement, a dance never forgotten
I've seen the world change, in ways beyond measure
A sad melody of destruction that needs to change
for the better

I've seen the seas rise, a heaving of the waves
A song of sorrow, a warning for our future days
I've witnessed the forests weep, as trees stand in despair
A requiem of nature, carried by the polluted air

But amidst the sorrow, there's still hope
A chance to heal, a way to cope
For though humans have done harm, they can
make amends
And work towards a future, that never ends

Let us all be the wind, a force so bold
A way to move forward, a beacon to hold
In the path of progress, forging our way
A current of change, with each passing day

Let's work together, to heal the earth
To protect our future, to show what it's worth
For we are the wind, a force to be reckoned
A symphony of movement, a dance never forgotten.

Olivia Eze (13)
Townley Grammar School For Girls, Bexleyheath

It Ends With Us

A walk in the park on a nice summer day,
Hand in hand, all the way.
The weather is pure and warm,
But it was as they always say,
The calm before the storm.

A quick glance he takes,
In the blink of an eye.
As he turns to look
At the passersby.

A second too long,
They catch each other's eye.
Deep inside she felt the fright.

Anniversary night,
What a loving sight.
If only he wasn't out tonight.

It's always "Not today, tomorrow or the day after that,"
His tone once full of love has now gone flat.
It seems the spark has faded out,
What has happened to who he once was?

2am he's up at night,
Who is he texting that gives him such delight?
The joy in his eyes she cannot bear to see,
The one that he wants, she knows she cannot be...

It seems we have grown,
Further and further apart.
Each step back we take,
Shatters more of my heart.

As I look over the bridge,
I think about how we used to be.
Joyful and in love,
Oh, how I miss thee.

It's time to end this grief and pain,
To finish off this tiring game.
One more step and I meet my fate,
Signing off, your once dear Kate...

Chanel Tumasang (13)
Townley Grammar School For Girls, Bexleyheath

Lemmings

Lemmings follow each other off cliffs,
They see one go down
And then they all go down, down, down
I heard that somewhere.

It doesn't make sense to me,
Because they must know
They must know who they're leaving
They must be someone, somewhere.

The young men come and they say,
"Surrender? Never Surrender!"
And we clench our shaking hands and we say,
"Surrender? Never Surrender!"

And the metal birds come and they lay their eggs,
And when the chicks are born, they blow
And the young shadows come and they say,
"Surrender!"

Up the steps to Marpi Point,
It feels like years since the sky was clear
The waves are crashing, crashing, crashing
I close my eyes and *breathe*.

Tumbling and ripping on the edges,
But nobody is screaming

One by one, we go
Like lemmings.

Martha Brown (12)
Townley Grammar School For Girls, Bexleyheath

Legacy

I want a legacy
Something long-lasting and great
Something to share with my kids when my hair turns grey.
I want a legacy.
Something to remember
Something to laugh about and pass on forever.
I want a legacy.
But I've got nothing to show.
I have written nothing upon the blank pages I tore.
Torn like the past, the present and the future
Forever forgotten and never to be remembered.
My words, my feelings, my emotions,
All spilt onto a frail piece of paper.
Too weak to hold such meaningful letters.
I have nothing to show.
My pain, my grief, my fear.
Things that only I feel
Too big to be described on my lined paper.
I have nothing to show, to share, to leave,
Afraid I'll have no words to spare by the time I leave.
I have no legacy, I never will,
I have nothing to show and most certainly nothing to tell.

Shaelyn Rayna (12)
Townley Grammar School For Girls, Bexleyheath

Who I Was

I gazed at my reflection
And tried to see your view
A stern, towering woman
With eyes of mesmerising blue

I reminisced about my youth and past
Old flashbacks and memories
A young, happy woman
Whistling under the trees

I went back to the day
You entered my life's door.
An excited, loving woman
That's who I was before.

I thought about the hard days
The smell of smoke in the air
A scared, mourning woman
Too much for me to bear

I looked deep inside
And struggled hard to see
The selfish, heartless mother
Is that what I came to be?

Deetya Tiwari (13)
Townley Grammar School For Girls, Bexleyheath

This Is Fame

Money
Fame
People love me
Crowds cheering for me
Apparently living the dream
This is not fame

Haters
Supporters
Those who don't care
This is fame

People judging
People criticising
People with crazy standards
This is fame

Fans
Super fans
Those who would go to any length
People on every corner
This is fame

No privacy
No respect
No personal space
Everyone knows everything about my life
This is fame

Constantly questioning myself
Should I do this?
Should I say this?
What will people think?
Will people still like me?
This is fame.

Maya Jheeta (12)
Townley Grammar School For Girls, Bexleyheath

The Fame

Safe and sound
I lie in bed
The outside screams
Pounding through my head

It's not raining today
I get up for a walk
And step outside my door
Only to hear the people talk

Screams from the crowd
Surrounding my front door
I smile and wave
It's nothing I haven't seen before

Flashing cameras blinds my eyes
"It's too early for this!"
I shout through the cries
And the paparazzi's lies

Bodies around me
Cheering my name
I don't want this
I don't want the fame.

Elise Kennard (13)
Townley Grammar School For Girls, Bexleyheath

Depths Of Heartache

In the depths of heartache, I find my way.
Grief and anger, emotions in disarray.
Friends once close, now distant and cold,
Leaving me feeling lost, a story untold.

Betrayed and gutted, my trust lies shattered.
But I won't let this pain leave me battered.
Through the tears and lows, I'll rise above,
Embracing the strength within, fuelled by love.

Heartache may linger but healing will come,
With time and self-care, I won't be undone.
Surrounded by those who lift me high,
I'll mend the wounds, spread my wings and fly.

Eva Topham (13)
Ysgol Brynhyfryd, Ruthin

Eternal Bliss

My life is not meaningless,
Or meaningful,
I try and try to pull away
From the harsh and dull.

Some days are tough,
Some days are rough
And some are not long enough.

I fall far down,
Into the depths of my mind,
It is hard to see, I cannot find

Myself, my mind, my empathy, my sadness
Everything is gone.
I dig deeper and deeper yet, I cannot see
Where they might be.

But, my friends and family,
Are there to help,
To be my guide, my compass
To eternal bliss.

Maya Venkat (12)
Ysgol Brynhyfryd, Ruthin

The Lively Mind And The Bright Leaves

Here, there, everywhere,
The wind swirls around, around.
Time is so precious.

So bright leaves hold hands.
Whoosh! They fly so low, so high.
Now it's time to rest.

Sonia Wasela (12)
Ysgol Brynhyfryd, Ruthin

Ode To Sports

A boy called Ethan, bold but not neat
Loved rugby and boxing; quite a feat!
With a ruck and a try
In boxing was spry
But in the scrum, young Ethan just couldn't be beat.

Ethan Mould (12)
Ysgol Brynhyfryd, Ruthin

YoungWriters® Est. 1991

YOUNG WRITERS INFORMATION

We hope you have enjoyed reading this book – and that you will continue to in the coming years.

If you're a young writer who enjoys reading and creative writing, or the parent of an enthusiastic poet or story writer, do visit our website **www.youngwriters.co.uk**. Here you will find free competitions, workshops and games, as well as recommended reads, a poetry glossary and our blog. There's lots to keep budding writers motivated to write!

If you would like to order further copies of this book, or any of our other titles, then please give us a call or order via your online account.

Young Writers
Remus House
Coltsfoot Drive
Peterborough
PE2 9BF
(01733) 890066
info@youngwriters.co.uk

Join in the conversation!
Tips, news, giveaways and much more!

YoungWritersUK **YoungWritersCW**
youngwriterscw **youngwriterscw**